A Concise Biography of

poems

John Samuel Tieman

Roy Fox Memorial Chapbook Series No. 5

BkMk Press
University of Missouri-Kansas City

BkMk Press
University of Missouri-Kansas City
5101 Rockhill Road
Kansas City, Missouri 64110
(816) 235-2558 (voice) / (816) 235-2611 (fax)
www.umkc.edu/bkmk

Financial assistance for this project has been provided by the
Missouri Arts Council, a state agency.

Cover art and author photo: Sheila Kennedy
Book design: Susan L. Schurman
Managing editor: Ben Furnish

BkMk Press wishes to thank Elizabeth Gromling, George Herndon, and
Jedsen Williams.

Printed in the United States of America.

Roy Fox Memorial Chapbook Series no. 5.
This series honors a founder of BkMk Press.

Library of Congress Cataloging-in-Publication Data

Tieman, John Samuel
     A concise biography of original sin / by John Samuel Tieman.
        p. cm.
     Summary: "Twenty poems confront human failure, vengeance, death,
disability, and grief, drawing meaning and solace from vivid descriptions of war
experiences, especially Vietnam and a veteran's life afterward"--Provided by publisher.
     ISBN 978-1-886157-73-6 (pbk. : alk. paper)
     I. Title.
     PS3620.I35C66 2009
     811'.6--dc22
                                        2009028323

This book is set in Stingwire, Techno, and Palatino typefaces.

for Phoebe

Acknowledgements

The author thanks Michael Simms for his kindness, his patience, his poetic and editorial insight, and, above all, his decades of profound friendship.

The author wishes to credit the following journals, broadcasts, magazines and newspapers where the following poems appeared.

"At My Wall's War": *Peace Talk, The Pittsburgh Quarterly OnLine* and *Drumvoices Revue.*
"The Child in White": *The Griffin, Broadside* and *The Pittsburgh Quarterly OnLine.*
"Clean": *Inside Recovery, The Pittsburgh Quarterly OnLine.*
"Dialogue with the Retired Marine": *River King Poetry Supplement.*
"Editing": *The Pittsburgh Quarterly OnLine.*
"for her brother": *Hawai'i Review.*
"4 AM": *The Iowa Review.*
"how to go blind": *English Journal.*
"if asked to judge": *Modern English Tanka.*
"Instead of a Eulogy": *The Chariton Review.*
"In this dream": *The American Psychoanalyst* and *Arabesques Review.*
"Lament in D-minor": *Friends Journal, U. News, The Pittsburgh Quarterly OnLine* and TV Channel 3 in Zagreb, Croatia.
"Passchendaele": *Webster Review, Peace Talk, The Pittsburgh Quarterly OnLine* and recorded by the Imperial War Museum, London.
"Punching-in": *Cimarron Review.*
"War Story": *The Pittsburgh Quarterly OnLine* and *Cimarron Review.*
"When Sgt. Nguyen Tri Lai Died": *Espejo.*
"With Regard to Auden": *Concho River Review.*

A Concise Biography of Original Sin

poems

Between me and my God
There are only eleven commandments;
The eleventh says: Thou shalt not
Bury thy brother alive
—Atukwei Okai

if asked to judge
my age I'd say we wasted
our best years on war
from Nam to Iraq we saw
the whole world through sniper scopes

A Concise Biography of Original Sin

I'll tell you a little horror story.
There's nothing people won't do.
We've seen the squad snap
at attention, heard the colonel
cry *Ready!*
and though we looked away,
we too took aim at the heart.
It's always been like this,
the muzzle, a puff of smoke,
someone muttering *Justice, justice* ...

You ask me why times are worse.
In just a moment of utter stupor
we ignore the beggar's gray sore,
ignore the slow tolling bell,
skim over articles on death.

I hear there's fresh air somewhere
or a woman I might someday love,
but here I smear my door with blood,
for wise men pray for the plague
and a black fog fills the streets.

Having failed in similar endeavors—

the 2nd wife, the last war, even
some tortures—the colonel turns

to you for help.
A single wick still flickers.

In a corner cell, there at the wall
your prisoner stares—the priest

for hours without a sound;
an executioner by shadow light

watching this one breathe
in, out.

But that's last night's story.
The creature is no more; now you

look weary, very weary from your work.

———————

Now climb the next rise and stand back.
See—who would have guessed?
Shadows so frail they fade,
a small boy plays a requiem
flute, ivory white, while you knot
promises of venom, chants, wet grass.

Editing

—for Denis Lane

This other Nam vet comes to see me and wants me to see
his manuscript.   He brings this nosh, some bagels, so I say
OK, let's see it—Yea, OK, I'll read it.   So we got some time till later so we swap
some Nam stories.   He says
This is what's pitiful, man.   I'm visitin' Jim Mills, this fuck-up all wounded you see.
It's this hospital, Nha Trang.   From a distance it's all this commotion.   But so what?
It's Nam.   I got directions to Jim Mills and I got to pass this commotion.   I start up
some stairs, begin to look a little into this
second floor when halfway up the flight I see nuthin' but runnin' feet and screams.
Just runnin' feet, some bunches of blood pools and some screams.   I got to turn
before I see completely in and there's the nurse all white right there
at the door.   I got to ask Hey What The Hell Lady? but she's just sittin', just
sittin' at this desk.   Imagine report
writin' at the door of the screams.   So I look.
The screams are a dozen guys—I can't tell black from whose white and they're all
runnin' and bangin' walls and leavin' whole body—I mean the full body on the wall
blood stains and they're naked 'cause all the napalm left was
no skin.   Nuthin'.   Not even no boots.
So I beg the nurse
Do Somethin'!   But she says Any More Morphine And They'll Die!   Finally I see
she's just as freaked and fakin' calm and nobody knows what to do so I go off on
her when one guy runs up at my face and he's just goin' Mama Mama Mama
Mama Mama Mama Mama Mama Mama Mama Mama Mama and like that.
(I always feel bad for that nurse 'cause she's maybe 23 and in charge of a
platoon of the dead or what's left.)   So I walk off, find some quiet and just stuff my
mouth with my fatigue shirt and scream till I can't stop.   And when Jim Mills later
asks What's that back there man? I say, you know how we said, Don't mean
nuthin', man.   It just don't mean nuthin'.

War Story

After I got out of the Nam
I made up some tales, some
mostly jokes—
One time we're tokin'—
One time the whores—
because nobody made any movies
about how we're heroes.
So now I'm told
You're a good guy, John,
Welcome Home, Pal!
So now I'll tell one
last story.   One night
on guard
I'm the new guy so
I decide I'd try my M-79.
Now an M-79 launches a grenade
a little farther than you can
hit a good home run.
Slow
I aim for this field.
Figure
range.
Bingo—a good shoot.
But the wind figures
in different, a freak
breeze
drifts the hit
into this village.
Where it kills this kid.
Except for the scream
that's the unadorned story.

—1987

When Sgt. Nguyen Tri Lai Died

I buried him in my sheet; I didn't have the heart
to kill some tree for a coffin.   After I flopped Lai
in the ragged hole I'd hacked, I decided to get dignified,
give him a one-gun salute.   You could tell
from those echoes and the empty shell case that fell
in his face that no one much missed him anyway.

At My War's Wall, a Vietnam Requiem in Which the Veteran Accepts the Dead

Your resurrection destroys all
our years of silence.   Still it
happens, a hang-round, Chi-Com grenade,
an AK maybe, RPG, these initials scribbled

in that last after-action report, your DD forms
that slam closed that file like this, that
silver casket.   Now your name forms part of a wall,
the final record, as if "Taps" is static.

As if my days groan on now
like some beast of burden
drawing the plow through the padi.
The padi has a name I remember

no one knows now, no one remembers
that my burden is a name, your name
simple as black granite—Hank,
Pete, Greaser.   No one speaks

as we spoke of home then, a woman,
a commune for dope-smoking Nam vets.
Our clothes clean.   Our skin healed.
Our languor brutal, brutal and pure.

I pause.   I walk away.
I am so alone, so alone
with the wall that became your name.
Let the years do with us as they will.

Let the birds of prey alight.
Who can kill you?
I will wear your name like a bracelet.
I will make flutes from your bones.

For a War Buddy After "Taps"

What can we say, buddy?
So much we could tell
we'll never tell—
the look of wheat after
we ate bullets to come home,

the look of a woman for who
you'd kill to love again,
the way the sun falls on
that patch, so they say,
nailed to the dink kid's skull.

Listen.   Maybe we'll say
What's it like, a theater
of war, I'll tell you: the hole
in his throat measured
only a fraction and tags

they IDed measured
say a square inch each;
the citation resembled
his diploma
and the VA donated

a simple modest slab;
some pals paid respects
from all across town
and all the way from LA
his fiancée.   Around the grave

they formed a circle of pain
that made infinity
small.   And I'll not measure
that last lament
heard only by God that night.

Or maybe we'll say—Listen!—we've
never seen a C-section
and cancer, but we've seen
this innocent kid in shreds
and we know it was no mistake.

Order of Battle

Indochina, 1970

First we map
     the coordinates
then we soften-up
     the village.
We begin by bombing
     the houses to pieces
then we bomb the pieces
     to rubble
then we bomb the rubble
     to bits
then we bomb the bits
     to ash.
Last we mop-up the leftover
     villagers
then we color Cambodia
     ours

Persian Gulf, 1991

First we map
     the coordinates
then we soften-up
     the enemy.
We begin by bombing
     the houses to pieces
then we bomb the pieces
     to rubble
then we bomb the rubble
     to bits
then we bomb the bits
     to ash.
Last we mop up the leftover
     draftees
then we color Kuwait
     ours

Punching-in

All history begins with
the Phoenicians
according to my teller.
Just a question of turning
profit.   Since then
we've lived civilized
as sacred objects
in an antique sale.
I'm reminded, I say,
of a simple account
the old Pole told
about the camp.
He was master
carpenter
and every morning
as a kind of joke, his capo
put him in line
for the oven;
and every morning, the main
merchant from town
plucked him up
just in time.
His town boss' problem was long
hours and that faulty
alarm.
According to the Jew
this is why
he's never late for work.

Lament in D-Minor

On the side-street outside a bakery everyday for 22
days at 4 PM in May 1993, Vedran Smailovic, a cellist
in the Sarajevo Symphony, played Albinoni's Adagio
for his brother plus 22 others killed by a mortar shell

Today it's all silence, the place
where the words must go.   A wail's diminuendo
to a gasp that never needs an explanation
that never knows another note, another measure

Like when there is only a hush
with a single lyric string praying
this is the way we practice sorrow
this is the way we practice death

22. 22. 22. The number ulcerates itself.
As a breeze tersely testifies to the space
between the pain and the adagio in the street
it makes us yearn for a definition of implosion

22. 22. The number multiplies each lament.
There was once a time for a theory of tragedy
how each crescendo culminates in the Phaedo
praying "How can we believe anything again"

22. Perhaps it means nothing, the number.
Perhaps the sorrow we know today is only a prelude
to the adagio we all call home, that place where
all the brothers and all their friends are lined

up against the wall, this wall that is the outline
for our sorrow.   Perhaps all sorrow is just a shell
aimed at all our side-streets where we are all lined up
for some bread, a chat, a song of someone's brother

A song in which slowly
we pray, pray
for another day, another
road, another brother, for this we pray

for her brother

wives get the word *widow*, husbands
widower, kids have *orphan*
but there's no word when there's a dead sister

only your own prayer composed for the moment
between the new wound and the opening pain
punctuated by an amen that implodes the soul

now that you've finished your house
you've got the time to tell her story over
and over to yourself, to anyone, to yourself

but if you could—the bullet out of her brain
and back in the barrel—the gun out of her hand
and back in the drawer—

but you can't
so the truth will just have to do
that and the family album, the rage and the slow letting go

how to go blind

there are maybe two ways around light
one is to close both eyes
the other my student tells me
she says my best cousin was tortured till he dies
his crime was being Albanian
I blind myself every night since I found him
stare into a bulb till it makes that little sun
that blots out his yellow black body

Dialogue with the Retired Marine

Did I ever see a man die?

The first time I saw this helicopter
rocket a clump of jungle, I saw
my whole world turn to gook gut

Would I speak with his mother?

I would.   I would explain
how her son died a hero by our
standards, how her son was

expensive and difficult to kill

The Child in White

C. S., 1978– 90
for her father

Ever since the war, something shrill
sings along your nerves, messages
like artillery coordinates

in a code no one knows.
Like the way lightening
clears the way for thunder

there are many ways to practice death.
Finding her body for one,
half-naked, the maniac

still in the neighborhood,
some guy you meet at the grocery.
For days the sun touched her teeth:

Not knowing how to stop
you remember her body
dead then alive then dead again.

The camera zooms in.
The reporter gets some fine lines but
your vow of vengeance pleases her most.

Who wouldn't grieve
the child in white,
who wouldn't grieve

as the prosecutor drags you
before the twelve elders
to recount the bruises

on her neck, on her thighs.
Who wouldn't grieve
as night after night

you strangle that bastard
over and over and over until
even his death isn't enough

death for the life of your daughter.
Now you too believe the evidence
of her azure lips

like all the other clues
the Major Case Squad missed:
The blood on the leaves,

the yellow frost, a fine ice.
You bear them as any father would bear
her empty room through the seasons

until they too turn
into a tender felon—
a winter, finally, of forgiveness.

With Regard to Auden

about war and all that, they get it
the old guys, Sassoon, Owen, all those
who understand it's as mundane as standing
guard, they understand

that it happens in some untidy country
where torturers work long hours
while the dictator confesses his most intimate sins and vows
from now on to stay faithful to the wife

in this old photo I shot in The Nam for example
how there's almost nothing there
except for the razor wire, a tower, an occasional Claymore mine
how everything seems perilously asleep

except for the kid in the bush
who is as implied
as the sniper, the painstaking aim
and the scream for which I had no recorder

Passchendaele

A man raves against God.   And war
among its faces
turns just one to you, the face
that is your own, your own.

It's not the kind of place that would worry
you in the usual June, your uniform manly,
your brass polished, sharp, so proud you
would recite your unit's history as if
it were a canto in its own Iliad.
But that was 1914, when freedom was measured
in the medals instead of the dead.

To look at it, there isn't much
of a ridge to speak of, 250 feet high,
its only claim to fame being
a splendid view of Flanders for which
544,897 die (maybe 4,700 a day)
give or take a half-dozen divisions.

What you have heard is true.
3:10 AM, 7 June 1917, Messines Ridge.
In preparation for the larger offensive,
1,000,000 lbs. of TNT detonated
along 5 mi. of galleries dug
under the Germans.   By 3:11 AM,
20,000 dead.   Survivors
mindless, infantile, gibbering.

The opening round.   Then Passchendaele,
a funeral cadence of muffled drums—
Hill 60, The Death Trench, Blood Chapel,
Ypres, Whitesheet, Hill 70, Goldfish
Chateau, the Vlamertinghe-Wipers Road—
a map no longer than a Mass card, requiem,
the litany of the dead angel of lead.
4,250,000 artillery shells fired
during the 1st 19 days alone.   Alone.
A fact.   And the fact of the matter is
simple: God is not on your side tonight.

And a man raves against God, earth,
man.   To think of you decomposing
even as you speak, humus once more,
once more a few pounds of ground,
earth, the many faces of earth, one
of which is a tomb and the tomb is
at once both earth and man.

Like vertigo, you twist into the earth
and beg the sun to blind you.   Instead
a sun spot burns a hole in a vision
you would kill if only you could
hang on till your mind gets right.

Who but a madman?   Who but a madman?
Who but a madman would have imagined mud
enough to die in?   Who but a madman would
put guns in the hands of all God's children,
tell them stories of glory then kill them?
Who but a madman would imagine Ypres salient?

A man raves against God.   And war
among its faces
turns just one to you, the face
which is your own, your own.

Your captain has his gas mask on,
standing near the sniper's nest,
advising the sergeant-major never
to show his face here again.
Your sniper has no face, no mask.   You
too will learn to burn out your eyes,
to take it like a man, to smother
under mud, to go mad like a man.

But what you thought was only darkness
has its own kind of light, like being
caught in a flare where the only terror
belongs to you: a German mortar crew
with nothing better to do than take aim
at you, just you, only you—there.

Besides the madness, there's the woman,
there's always the woman, delicate as a lie,
clean and white, someone the mud doesn't touch,
not someone who runs like the meaning
of speech, but a woman, a woman, your woman,
the one woman in the world who could save you.
The one woman in the world you wish to die with.

Adrenaline.   The word burns the very marrow.

In a moment no longer than a flare,
in the time it takes a scream to reach
Sweet Jesus, among a hundred dead, another,
another man trapped in mud, another man then

another, another sniper takes aim, another
bullet goes astray and finds a home, the heart,
and the bullet will burst like a mortar in the gut
and the gut will turn to lead and the lead
to the rain, always a slow assault of a rain,
speechless as incest, shrapnel like a rapist,
definite as barbed wire, permanent as the front,
always the past turns its face to ebony rain
and tomorrow will be just like today.

Note:
Following the capture of Messines Ridge, the Battle of Passchendaele, also known as
the Third Battle of Ypres, properly began on 31 July 1917 with a British push toward
the Belgian coast. After four months, the British penetrated a total of only five
miles into the German lines, this end point being the village of Passchendaele. The
Germans recaptured all this within six months. The British pronounce this place
"Passiondale."

Clean

Today 1/11/96 sober six years and
I say morning prayers without speaking
I make the coffee while my wife rises
I listen without weeping at a sad ballad

The sound of the snow on the roof is
important, important as fresh bread
or the neighbor warming her car
important as a plan or an empty chair

That's why this morning six years
later to the day I hear the slight
chimes of the Angelus bells hear
the ash settle in my fireplace

hear the beauty of my wife's sigh
as she sits cross-legged on the edge
of the bed and asks half-aware
why I'm alive at this hour

Instead of a Eulogy

When my father died, there was no dignity.   Only his inability to breathe
and my inability to speak.   Like two old houses, one dumb as stone.   The other
barely habitable.   No blessing of bread and blood, no forsaking
the silence for the crafted last word.   We were as we always were

the silence of men barely breathing, afraid to move or be still

But there was more.   When my father died, his mouth dropped
open.   So after I recite Psalm 51, after I pray God assume him, when I am
last alone with my father, I try to close that mouth.   But I can't.   Rigor
set in fast, so fast and so concrete

as if all the words we'd meant to say solidified

4 AM

I

like a leaf that wishes to drop
    at the foot of the tree and become, for the sake of the tree, some small feast
there is a life I long to give back
    like Li Po folding his poems and floating them downstream only to be
    retrieved by someone who loved poems perhaps or paper boats or just Li Po
there is something I wish to give my wife, something that is neither
yowl nor vow

II

my wife speaking in her sleep
speaks in a secret language like English but a glossolalia
known only to her and God and
    me as I marvel
my wife breathing in when
    she stops and for 7 seconds I know all there is to know
    about love and the meaning of love and loss and all there is to lose
    and she breathes again and again I know God
by her silence, for example, how my wife's silence is then
    how my wife's 4 AM silence is all I need of silence and God's gift of silence
    which is to say
    her skin amid all the dark

In this dream

there is food and water
and no barrier reef, only shore

this woman is my wife
the compass close enough

the uncertain current I understand
and I feel strangely safe sailing long after dark

still alive days after the disaster
everything I need within reach

Born in St. Louis, John Samuel Tieman has lived in Mexico City and the West Indies. He served with the U. S. Army in Vietnam. A certified teacher since 1975, he earned his Ph. D. from Saint Louis University. He teaches history and English in the St. Louis Public Schools. In addition to poetry, John Samuel Tieman has published essays in the *St. Louis Post-Dispatch*, *Los Angeles Times*, *Chicago Tribune*, *Des Moines Register*, *Kansas City Star*, *National Catholic Reporter*, *Stars and Stripes*, and elsewhere.